Lesson Planning

Nikki Ashcraft

English
Language
Teacher
Development
Series

Thomas S. C. Farrell,
Series Editor

Typeset in Janson and Frutiger
by Capitol Communications, LLC, Crofton, Maryland USA
and printed by Gasch Printing, LLC, Odenton, Maryland USA

TESOL Press
TESOL International Association
1925 Ballenger Avenue
Alexandria, Virginia 22314 USA

Publishing Manager: Carol Edwards
Cover Design: Tomiko Breland
Copyeditor: Tomiko Breland

TESOL Book Publications Committee
John I. Liontas, Chair
Robyn L. Brinks Lockwood, Co-chair   Guofang Li
Margo DelliCarpini   Gilda Martinez-Alba
Deoksoon Kim   Adrian J. Wurr
Ilka Kostka

Reviewer: Margo DelliCarpini

ISBN 9781942223351

Contents

About the Author

Nikki Ashcraft, PhD, has worked as a teacher educator in the United States, the United Arab Emirates, and Chile. She is currently an Assistant Teaching Professor in the online TESOL program at the University of Missouri, USA, where she enjoys interacting with preservice and in-service teachers around the world.

Series Editor's Preface

The English Language Teacher Development (ELTD) Series consists of a set of short resource books for English language teachers that are written in a jargon-free and accessible manner for all types of teachers of English (native and nonnative speakers of English, experienced and novice teachers). The ELTD series is designed to offer teachers a theory-to-practice approach to English language teaching, and each book offers a wide variety of practical teaching approaches and methods for the topic at hand. Each book also offers opportunities for teachers to interact with the materials presented. The books can be used in preservice settings or in in-service courses and can also be used by individuals looking for ways to refresh their practice.

Nikki Ashcraft's book *Lesson Planning* explores different approaches to planning lessons and the various challenges this may present to a language teacher. Nikki provides a comprehensive overview of lesson planning for the language classroom in an easy-to-follow guide that language teachers will find very practical for their own contexts. Topics covered include importance and approaches to planning, and details on the practice of planning. *Lesson Planning* is a valuable addition to the literature in our profession.

I am very grateful to the authors who contributed to the ELTD Series for sharing their knowledge and expertise with other TESOL professionals, because they have do so willingly without any compensation to make these short books affordable to all language teachers throughout the world. It is truly an honor for me to work with each of these authors as they selflessly gave up their valuable time for the advancement of TESOL.

Thomas S. C. Farrell

1

The Importance of Planning

Lesson planning is at the heart of being an effective teacher. It is a creative process that allows us to synthesize our understanding of second language acquisition and language teaching pedagogy with our knowledge of our learners, the curriculum, and the teaching context. It is a time when we envision the learning we want to occur and analyze how all the pieces of the learning experience should fit together to make that vision a classroom reality.

There are a number of benefits to writing a lesson plan. First, lesson planning produces more unified lessons (Jensen, 2001). It gives teachers the opportunity to think deliberately about their choice of lesson objectives, the types of activities that will meet these objectives, the sequence of those activities, the materials needed, how long each activity might take, and how students should be grouped. Teachers can reflect on the links between one activity and the next, the relationship between the current lesson and any past or future lessons, and the correlation between learning activities and assessment practices. Because the teacher has considered these connections and can now make the connections explicit to learners, the lesson will be more meaningful to them.

The lesson planning process allows teachers to evaluate their own knowledge with regards to the content to be taught (Reed & Michaud, 2010). If a teacher has to teach, for example, a complex grammatical structure and is not sure of the rules, the teacher would become aware of this during lesson planning and can take steps to acquire the necessary information. Similarly, if a teacher is not sure how to pronounce a new vocabulary word, this can be remedied during the lesson planning process. The opportunity that lesson planning presents to evaluate one's own knowledge is particularly advantageous for teachers of English for specific purposes, because these teachers have to be not only language experts, but also familiar with different disciplines like business, engineering, or law—fields that use language in specialized ways.

A teacher with a plan, then, is a more confident teacher (Jensen, 2001). The teacher is clear on what needs to be done, how, and when. The lesson will tend to flow more smoothly because all the information has been gathered and the details have been decided upon beforehand. The teacher will not waste class time flipping through the textbook, thinking of what to do next, or running to make photocopies. The teacher's confidence will inspire more respect from the learners, thereby reducing discipline problems and helping the learners to feel more relaxed and open to learning.

Some teachers feel that lesson planning takes too much time. Yet lesson plans can be used again, in whole or in part, in other lessons months or years in the future (Jensen, 2001). Many teachers keep files of previous lessons they have taught, which they then draw on to facilitate planning for their current classes. In other words, lesson planning now can save time later.

Lesson plans can be useful for other people as well (Jensen, 2001). Substitute teachers face the challenge of teaching another teacher's class and appreciate receiving a detailed lesson plan to follow. Knowing that the substitute is following the plan also gives the regular classroom teacher confidence that the class time is being used productively in his or her absence. In addition, lesson plans can also document for administrators the instruction that is occurring. If a supervisor wants to know what was done in class two weeks ago, the teacher only has to refer to that day's lesson plan. Finally, lesson plans can serve as evidence of a teacher's professional performance. Teachers are sometimes asked to include lesson plans, along with other materials, as part of a portfolio to support their annual performance evaluation. Teachers applying for new jobs might be asked to submit lesson plans as part of their job application so that employers can get a sense of their organizational skills and teaching style.

This book will lead you through the lesson planning process and highlight the role of the plan before, during, and after your lesson. The next chapter presents some approaches to lesson planning while the third chapter outlines the practical considerations involved in the process. Reflective Break segments pose questions to help you apply the information in this book to your own teaching practice.

REFLECTIVE BREAK

Think of a time you entered a class with a hastily written lesson plan or no plan at all.

- How did you feel?

- How would the lesson have been improved with more thorough planning?

2

Approaches to Planning

The process of lesson planning can be approached in several ways. Forward, central, and backward design are approaches to curriculum development that are also applicable to lesson planning. Universal Design for Learning intends to address individual differences in learners and to remove barriers to their learning.

Forward, Central, and Backward Design

Forward, *central*, and *backward* design refer to the starting point of the planning process and how the process develops. With a forward design process, the teacher begins by identifying the linguistic or cultural content to be taught. He or she then decides upon the methods and activities to be used to teach this content and ends with the assessment of learning. For instance, the teacher might see that the syllabus calls for teaching language related to the topic of travel. The teacher decides to use pictures to present travel-related vocabulary and have students practice travel-related dialogues from their textbook. The assessment, which is an end-of-semester exam, requires students to match vocabulary words and definitions and to fill in the blanks in a travel-themed paragraph.

> *A forward design option may be preferred in circumstances where a mandated curriculum is in place, where teachers have little choice over what and how to teach, where teachers rely mainly on textbooks and commercial materials rather than teacher-designed resources, where class size is large and where tests and assessments are designed centrally rather than by individual teachers. (Richards, 2013, p. 29)*

A weakness of this approach, though, is that covering the syllabus or finishing the textbook may take precedence over actual learning (Wiggins & McTighe, 2005).

A central design process starts with the teacher making decisions regarding methods and activities. Once these have been selected, the content of the lesson and the learning outcomes are derived from there. "Learning is not viewed as the mastery of pre-determined content but as constructing new knowledge through participating in specific learning and social contexts and through engaging in particular types of activities and processes" (Richards, 2013, p. 19). This approach to lesson planning allows teachers a lot of autonomy.

> *Teaching strategies are developed according to the teacher's understanding of the context in which he or she is working as well as on his or her individual skill and expertise in managing the instructional process and in developing teaching materials and forms of assessment. (Richards, 2013, p. 29)*

For example, the teacher may decide to use a group ranking task with students because this would generate a lot of discussion. The ranking task would require students to express opinions using language like "I think" or "In my opinion." It would also require students to use ordinal numbers and comparative structures. Therefore, the teacher determines that the content of this lesson is expressing opinions, using ordinal numbers, and comparing items. After the lesson has been taught, the assessment is created to evaluate the use of these forms and functions. Wiggins and McTighe (2005), however, critique the central design process as being "'hands-on without being minds-on'— engaging experiences that lead only accidentally, if at all, to insight or achievement" (p. 16).

In the backwards design process, the first step is for the teacher to identify the end result of the lesson. Having participated in the lesson, "what should students know, understand, and be able to do?" (Wiggins & McTighe, 2005, p. 17). From there, the teacher determines the sort of evidence that would prove this learning has occurred. In other words, the teacher thinks ahead to the forms of assessment that could measure this learning. Only then, after elaborating the goals of the lesson and considering assessment evidence, does the teacher turn to making decisions about the learning activities. To illustrate, the teacher would identify (perhaps by conducting a needs analysis or by referring to a set of standards adopted by his or her school) that students need to be able to describe a process orally and in writing. This would become the objective for the lesson. Next, the teacher would think of how describing a process could be assessed and may actually write the question prompts and the rubric for the final assessment at this time. Finally, the teacher would determine which classroom activities students could engage in that would prepare them to achieve the objectives and successfully complete the assessment. Richards (2013) notes that "a backward design option may be preferred in situations where a high degree of accountability needs to be built into the curriculum design and where resources can be committed to needs analysis, planning, and materials development" (p. 29).

REFLECTIVE BREAK

- Do you currently use a forward, central, or backward design process when planning your lessons?

- Think of a lesson you have recently implemented. How was that lesson influenced by your design process?

- How might that lesson have turned out differently had it been planned using one of the other approaches?

Universal Design for Learning

Another approach to lesson planning is encapsulated in the three principles of Universal Design for Learning (UDL), a model of lesson and curricula development which emphasizes creating equal opportunity for all students to learn, regardless of any physical, cognitive, or linguistic limitations. These three principles are for teachers to "provide multiple means of representation," "multiple means of action and expression," and "multiple means of engagement" (Center for Applied Special Technology, 2011, p. 5; see Figure 1).

The first principle of UDL (see Figure 1) is to "provide multiple means of representation" because "learners differ in the ways that they perceive and comprehend information that is presented to them"

(Center for Applied Special Technology, 2011, p. 5). This includes providing options for learners to perceive information, for instance, by presenting the same information through the different modalities of sight, sound, and touch. The field of TESOL has long promoted the use of visual aids, such as pictures and realia, and kinaesthetic activities, such as total physical response, or TPR, to facilitate language learning (Brown, 2007). Presenting the information through these different modalities allows learners to not only better comprehend the information but also make stronger connections between concepts. Another example of providing options for perception is giving information to learners in formats that they can control and adjust. For instance, when a teacher plays (or reads) a listening text for the whole class, it is the teacher who controls the volume, speed, and number of repetitions. Yet if students listen to the text on individual audio players, they can listen to the text as many times as they need to, control the volume, and possibly even the speed of the recording. The first principle of UDL also includes providing learners with options for how language, mathematical expressions, and symbols are represented. For those teachers who teach English language learners in content-based classes such as math or science, this principle of UDL implies that they will need to devote time to teaching vocabulary, simplifying the grammar in the information presented to students, and possibly even presenting some information in the learners' first language in order to make the content comprehensible to them. This principle further encompasses providing learners with options for how they comprehend information. Building and activating learners' schema on a new topic and teaching them how to use learning strategies are ways teachers can enact this element of the first principle.

REFLECTIVE BREAK

Think of a lesson you will teach in the near future.
- How can you address the different ways that learners perceive and comprehend information in this lesson?

Principle I. Provide Multiple Means of Representation
Provide options for
- perception
- language, mathematical expressions, and symbols
- comprehension

Principle II. Provide Multiple Means of Action and Expression
Provide options for
- physical action
- expression and communication
- executive functions

Principle III. Provide Multiple Means of Engagement
Provide options for
- recruiting interest
- sustaining effort and persistence
- self-regulation

Figure 1. Universal Design for Learning Principles (Center for Applied Special Technology, 2011)

The second principle of UDL (see Figure 1) is to "provide multiple means of action and expression" as "learners differ in the ways that they can navigate a learning environment and express what they know" (Center for Applied Special Technology, 2011, p. 5). This includes providing different options for physical actions, in the case of learners with physical disabilities. For instance, learners who are physically unable to write or type may use speech to text software to create their assignments. This principle also involves allowing for alternative modalities of expression, such as speaking, writing, drawing by hand, sculpting, and creating with digital media. This aspect of the second principle is particularly important when working with beginning language learners in content-area classes. These learners may have understanding of the content but lack the language proficiency to express their knowledge in English. Therefore, allowing them the option of demonstrating their knowledge through modalities that do not involve language, such as drawing or miming, allows them to more fully participate in the lesson.

Similarly, offering activities with various levels of scaffolding permits lower proficiency students to participate just as higher proficiency students do. For example, a dictation exercise can be adapted for students at different proficiency levels by giving less proficient students a text with a few blanks to fill in, giving more proficient students a text with more blanks to fill in, and asking the most proficient students to write the entire paragraph. This third principle also involves providing options for executive functioning. This relates to developing learners' abilities to set learning goals, plan their learning, choose appropriate learning tools and strategies, and monitor their own progress. Developing learners' use of language learning strategies, including metacognitive strategies, has long been of interest in the field of TESOL, and many resources have been published in this area (see, for example, Oxford, 2011).

REFLECTIVE BREAK

Think of a lesson you will teach in the near future.

- How can you provide learners with different ways of navigating the learning environment and expressing what they know in this lesson?

The third principle of UDL (see Figure 1) is to "provide multiple means of engagement." This refers to the role of affect in learning and the fact that "learners differ markedly in the ways in which they can be engaged or motivated to learn" (Center for Applied Special Technology, 2011, p. 5). This principle includes stimulating learners' interest in various ways. For instance, learners can be given choices in the types of activities they do, the tools they use, or the rewards they will receive. Learners should be presented with activities that are relevant to their goals and that are culturally and age appropriate. Also, learners should feel physically and emotionally safe in the learning environment.

Another aspect of this third principle is the ways in which learners are motivated to sustain their effort and persist in achieving their goals. Teachers may remind learners of their goals by having the goals posted in the class and discussing with them periodically the progress they have made. Creating cooperative learning groups allows learners to help and encourage each other (see discussion of grouping in Chapter 3). Furthermore, learners' motivation to continue learning is enhanced when they receive frequent feedback that emphasizes their development.

The third principle also involves fostering learners' self-regulation of their emotions and motivation. This is accomplished by helping learners to set realistic goals, to monitor their progress, and to think positively about what they can do, rather than about what they cannot yet do. Understanding and enhancing motivation to learn a second/foreign language has been a primary concern in the field of TESOL (see, for example, Dörnyei & Ushioda, 2010); thus, the UDL principle of using multiple strategies for motivating students is particularly relevant for ESL/EFL teachers.

REFLECTIVE BREAK

Think of a lesson you will teach in the near future.

- What steps could you take to stimulate your students' motivation in this lesson?

UDL does not give teachers a step-by-step process for lesson planning, yet it does have implications for evaluating and planning "goals, methods, materials, and assessments for the purpose of creating a fully accessible learning environment for all" (Center for Applied Special Technology, 2011, p. 13).

3

The Practice of Planning

As language teachers create, implement, and reflect on their lesson plans, they draw upon all of their professional knowledge and experience. They think about theoretical principles of second language acquisition, like the role of comprehensible input and students' motivations for learning a language (Brown, 2007), and about their own beliefs on how acquisition occurs. They think about best practices for teaching reading, writing, listening, speaking, grammar, and vocabulary. And perhaps predominately, they think about the characteristics of the learners in their class; the curriculum or textbook they have been given to teach; the cultural and institutional context in which they work; and the availability of and constraints on resources like time, space, and materials. All of this knowledge informs the decisions teachers make as they write their lesson plans, implement (and deviate from) those plans in the classroom, and evaluate the success of those plans once the lesson is over.

Creating Your Plan

Lesson plans can take many forms. They may be handwritten or typed. They may be printed on paper or only exist electronically. Some schools ask their teachers to use a particular template for lesson planning. Regardless of its form, every plan should contain certain elements. These are your lesson objectives, the procedures you will follow, a listing of the materials you will need, an indication of how you plan to assess students' learning, and a notation of any out-of-class work you expect students to complete. As you read about the different elements of the lesson plan below, please refer to the sample plan in the appendix. See lesson plan resources at the end of the Reference section.

Objectives

The role of objectives in the lesson planning process depends on whether the teacher's approach to lesson planning reflects a forward, central, or backward design (see Chapter 2). In forward design, objectives determine the activities, which in turn lead to the assessment. In central design, objectives emerge from the selection of learning activities. In backward design, the objectives are essential to developing the assessment, which then has an influence on the types of activities that are employed (Richards, 2013). In any case, objectives are an essential component of your plan, giving purpose and direction to your lesson.

Where do objectives come from? How do you know what learners need to know, and therefore, what you should teach them? If your school has adopted a set of curriculum standards, if a syllabus has been designed for your course, or if a textbook has been provided, then you should refer to these documents to determine which language forms, functions, skills, and learning strategies your learners need to develop. If no such documents are available, then you will need to conduct a needs analysis to investigate what your learners need to know about and be able to do with language. A needs analysis involves gathering information about the learners' language learning needs through surveys and interviews with the learners; observations of the learners as they interact with English speakers; surveys and interviews with employers (in the case of adult learners); examination of the kinds of texts that the learners need to read and write; and review of the learners' previous classwork or the results of diagnostic, placement, achievement, or proficiency tests they have taken. For more details on the process of conducting a needs analysis, please refer to Richards (2001).

A language lesson may have only one or two objectives or several objectives, depending on the length of the lesson. However, teachers need to be realistic about the number of objectives that students can achieve in one lesson period. Objectives should be written from the perspective of what students will do during the lesson. In addition, they should be observable and measurable (Reed & Michaud, 2010). For instance, writing "The teacher will present simple past tense" is not a well-written objective because it tells what the teacher will do rather than what the students will do. Writing "The students will learn simple past tense" has put the focus on the student, yet what does "learn" mean in terms of student behavior? The action is not observable and could be difficult to measure. Verbs like "learn," "know" and "understand" should be replaced with verbs that reflect observable and measure actions (see examples listed in Figure 2).

Language objectives can cover any aspect of language. For instance, objectives may focus on particular language forms (i.e., words, sounds, or grammatical structures).

Examples: Learners will orally identify the members in a family using the words <u>mother</u>, <u>father</u>, <u>wife</u>, <u>husband</u>, <u>son</u>, <u>daughter</u>, <u>brother</u>, and <u>sister</u>.

Learners will compare/contrast two animals in writing using <u>comparative adjectives</u>.

The language objectives might emphasize specific language functions that students will perform.

Examples: Learners will orally <u>express their opinions</u> on the new highway proposal.

Learners will write an e-mail to their landlord <u>complaining</u> about a maintenance issue.

act out/dramatize	evaluate	perform
analyze	explain	predict
categorize	give examples of	rank
choose/select	identify	read
classify	infer	say/state
compare/contrast	label	summarize
count	list	tell/relate/report
create	locate	write (instructions,
define	match	a letter, a
describe	order	paragraph,
draw	paraphrase	sentences)

Figure 2. Verbs That Represent Observable and Measurable Actions

The language objectives may highlight how students will use one of the four language skills.

Examples: Learners will <u>listen</u> to a lecture and identify the main ideas.

Learners will preview the subtitles and pictures in a <u>reading</u> passage and make predictions about the text.

The language objectives could deal with developing pragmatic usage of the language.

Examples: Learners will demonstrate <u>politeness</u> in responding to an invitation, either accepting it ("Thank you.") or refusing it ("I'm sorry. I'm busy that day.").

Learners will demonstrate <u>respect</u> when making suggestions to a superior by using modals (may, might, would, could).

Finally, the language objectives could describe the learners' use of language learning strategies.

Examples: Learners will <u>take notes on the main ideas</u> in the listening passage.

Learners will <u>use an online dictionary</u> to look up unknown words in the reading passage.

Brown (2007) explains the difference between terminal objectives and enabling objectives. Terminal objectives are those which will be achieved by the end of the lesson. These are the objectives that will be covered by the assessment. However, sometimes other learning needs to occur before those terminal objectives can be met. This learning is described by enabling objectives. For example, before learners can "compare/contrast two animals in writing using comparative adjectives" (terminal objective), learners will need to be able to identify the names of animals, describe the animals, and state some facts about them (enabling objectives). Whether you will need to write both terminal objectives and enabling objectives in your plan, or whether terminal objectives alone are sufficient, depends on the protocol at your school.

If you are teaching English language learners using a content-based instruction approach or content and language integrated learning, you will need to establish both language objectives and content objectives for your lesson. Like language objectives, content objectives need to describe what students will do and be observable and measurable. Ideally, there would be a relationship between the content objective and the language objective(s).

Examples: (Content Objective)
- Learners will explain the reasons for the U.S. Civil War.

(Language Objectives)
- Learners will accurately use simple past tense to write and talk about the U.S. Civil War.

- Learners will define vocabulary related to the U.S. Civil War (e.g., *civil, secession, confederacy, slavery, abolitionist, emancipation, proclamation*).

- Learners will use suffixes (-ion, -ist) to determine a word's part of speech.

- Learners will present a clear thesis statement in the introductory paragraph of their essay and clear topic sentences in each supporting paragraph.

For more information on the relationship between language objectives and content objectives, see Echevarría, Vogt, and Short (2013).

If your school adheres to any curriculum standards, you may also be asked to indicate in your lesson plan which curriculum standards your lesson addresses (Jensen, 2001). This information would appear in the objectives section of your plan because your lesson objectives would be closely tied to fulfilling those standards.

REFLECTIVE BREAK

Look at the objectives from a lesson you have recently taught.

- Are the objectives observable, measureable, and written from the perspective of what the learners will do? If not, what changes could you make to improve the objectives?

- Do your language objectives tend to focus on language form, function, skills, pragmatic use, or learning strategies?

Procedures

The procedures section of the lesson plan will be the longest section of the plan. It describes what the teacher and students will do during the lesson. In planning your procedures, you will make decisions about the kinds of activities that will occur during the lesson and the order in which those activities will be carried out. Here, it is best to think through the lesson thoroughly and to provide as much detail as possible. For example, in addition to describing the activities, some teachers like to script out the instructions, explanations, and examples they will provide students (Brown, 2007).

Sequencing   A good way to begin your lesson is to briefly inform students about the objectives of the lesson (Echevarría, Vogt, & Short, 2013). These should be written in simple language that learners can understand, and shown to them on the board, on a poster, or on a slide. Knowing the objectives of the lesson can help students feel more secure in the class because they will know what is coming ahead. It can stimulate their interest in the lesson and activate their previous knowledge of the content. Having the objectives visible to learners also serves to keep the lesson on track. If students make comments that are off topic or ask questions that are beyond their proficiency level, the teacher can always point to the objectives and say, "I'm sorry. That question does not relate to our objectives today. We can talk about that in another class."

There are many possibilities for sequencing the other activities in your lesson. For instance, activities where students use the receptive skills of reading and listening usually occur before those requiring the productive skills of speaking and writing. Easier activities often build up to more complex, more difficult activities (Richards & Lockhart, 1996). Traditionally, it has been common for a language lesson to follow the Presentation-Practice-Production model. In this model, the teacher first presents a specific language form or function to the learners, giving an explanation and examples. Then, students practice the form or function in a controlled way, perhaps in a drill or fill-in-the-blank exercise. Finally, students have the opportunity to produce language more freely in a communicative activity (Willis & Willis, 2007).

The structure of the lesson plan may be influenced by the skill focus of the lesson. For example, lesson plans whose objectives are to develop listening and reading skills are often organized according to a pre-skill practice, during-skill practice, and post-skill practice framework. In the prelistening/reading stage, students' interest in the topic of the listening/reading text is stimulated and their schemata on the content and the text type is activated. In the during-listening/reading stage, students practice the language skill and apply strategies such as guessing words from context and identifying main ideas to aid their comprehension. In the postlistening/reading stage, students demonstrate their comprehension of the text and use information from the text to complete other tasks (Flowerdew & Miller, 2005; Grabe &

Stoller, 2001). Teachers who teach writing using a process approach would organize their lesson using activities that guide students through the stages of the writing process: prewriting (including brainstorming and selecting ideas), drafting the text, getting feedback on the text, revising the ideas in the text, and editing the text for language (Brown, 2007). See other volumes in the English Language Teacher Development Series for further information on teaching listening (Nemtchinova, 2013) reading (Day, 2013), and writing (Tomaš, Kostka, & Mott-Smith, 2013).

Newer approaches to language teaching, such as task-based teaching, propose a unique sequence of activities. In task-based teaching, the lesson is built around students' completion of a task where the focus is on the communication of meaning rather than the use of a particular form or function. This task should be interesting to learners and connected to real-world activities. It should have a final outcome such as creating a product, like a poster, or making a decision. Priority is given to students' completing the task and achieving this outcome. It is only after students have completed the task that attention turns to analyzing the language they used to fulfill it (Willis & Willis, 2007).

Another way of organizing your lesson is using the flipped model. "Basically the concept of a flipped class is this: that which is traditionally done in class is now done at home, and that which is traditionally done as homework is now completed in class" (Bergmann & Sams, 2012, p. 13). Instead of lecturing and presenting new concepts in class, the teacher provides materials (often in video format) explaining the new concepts for students to read, view, and review outside of class. This frees up class time so that, when students come to class, they spend the majority of their time working on exercises and engaging in activities to apply the concepts. In the case of a language classroom, this means more time spent actually using the language. The teacher's role is to monitor, assist, and assess students as they are working. Bergmann and Sams (2012) discuss the advantages of the flipped classroom model and provide practical tips for implementation.

Reflective Break

- Which of the classroom activities you commonly use could be performed by students outside of class? Which require the support of the teacher and/or interaction with classmates?

- Think of a lesson you have recently implemented. How could that lesson be flipped?

At the end of your class time, you should plan to allot a few minutes to bring the lesson to a close (Richards & Lockhart, 1996). This step of the lesson's procedure is often neglected. Teachers run out of class time, or they have not deliberately thought through how they would end the lesson. However, the last few minutes of the lesson offer a prime opportunity to synthesize the learning that has occurred and make connections between this lesson and other lessons. You (or the students) can review the objectives again to recall what was accomplished during the lesson. You can then give students a preview of what the next lesson will cover. Some teachers ask students to complete exit slips during this time. Exit slips may contain a question related to the content of the day's lesson (e.g., "How could you politely ask someone to close the door?"). Exit slips might ask students to provide the teacher with feedback on the lesson by responding to questions like "What was the lesson about? Which part of the lesson was easy? Which part of the lesson was difficult?" Additionally, the exit slip could present a reflective sentence prompt, such as "Today I learned _____" or "I am confused about _____," which stimulates students to think about their own learning. Exit slips are a useful tool, then, for informally assessing students' learning, evaluating our lessons, and fostering students' metacognitive awareness.

When discussing procedure, it is also useful to consider the use of classroom routines (Scrivener, 2012). A classroom routine is an activity that is performed regularly in exactly the same way. For example, a teacher of young learners might open every lesson by having students stand and sing the "Good Morning" song. A teacher of older learners might ask students to spend 15 minutes during each lesson writing in a dialogue journal or engaging in extensive reading. The exit slips mentioned above could also become part of a routine. Developing a few classroom routines assists in lesson planning because the teacher knows that these activities will always be included and the steps have already been predetermined. Having a few classroom routines also helps with classroom management, especially with younger and lower proficiency students. With routines, students know what to expect and what to do, and so feel less anxious about participating in class. Also, because students already know the procedure, the teacher can spend less time giving instructions and students can spend more time actually completing the activity. Teachers should be warned, though, against making the entire lesson one long routine. Incorporating a variety of activities, including new activities, helps maintain students' interest and motivation (Brown, 2007; Jensen, 2001).

As you can see from the variety of lesson structures discussed above, there is no one way to organize your lesson. Your choice of lesson structure will depend on the goals of your lesson, what is acceptable at your school, and what is effective for you and your students.

REFLECTIVE BREAK

- How do you usually sequence the activities in your lessons?

- Why do you sequence the activities in this way?

Timing   As you plan out your procedures, think about the length of your class period and estimate how long each activity would take. This is important for ensuring that you make effective use of the entire class period, and also for keeping your expectations realistic in terms of what can be accomplished in a limited amount of time. Beginning proficiency students will engage in simpler activities that may be completed more quickly; therefore, a plan for students of this proficiency level will probably consist of a larger number of short (5–15 minute) activities. More proficient students can engage in more complex activities, which may require various steps. Because these activities take more time, fewer activities would be necessary. Another consideration with regards to estimating time is the age and attention span of your learners. Younger learners are better served with a greater variety of shorter activities while older learners have the ability to engage in activities that require concentration for longer periods of time (Brown, 2007).

Grouping A final consideration as you develop the procedural part of your lesson plan is how students will be grouped in each activity. Will students participate as a whole class, in large or small groups, in pairs, or individually? Using different formats during the lesson provides variety and helps maintain students' interest. In addition, pair and group activities present opportunities for interaction and negotiation of meaning, which are essential for second language acquisition to occur (Lightbown & Spada, 2013). If you decide that an activity is best completed by students in groups, you will need to decide how many students would be the optimal number for each group. For instance, if you have 20 students, you might decide to have students work in five groups with four students each. Remember that the larger the group, the fewer opportunities there will be for each student to participate and the harder it may be for the group to come to a consensus, if that is what the activity requires. Once you have decided upon the type of student formation, you will then need to determine how those pairs or groups will be formed. These are some possible ways of forming pairs or groups:

- assigning partners based on similar proficiency levels
- assigning partners based on differing proficiency levels (e.g., one higher proficiency and one lower proficiency student)
- assigning partners who share the same first language
- assigning partners who have different first languages
- assigning partners based on their personalities (e.g., extroverts, introverts)
- assigning partners based on other characteristic such as age or gender
- using a system (e.g., drawing names from a bag) or an activity (like the plan in the appendix) that would create random pairs/ groups of students

- asking students to work with a classmate near them

- letting students choose their own partners (Brown, 2007)

For a detailed discussion on the use of pair and group activities in language teaching, see Jacobs and Kimura (2013).

REFLECTIVE BREAK

- How do you usually form pairs/groups in your classes?

- What are the advantages and disadvantages of each of the methods for pair/group formation listed above?

Materials

Once you have decided upon the activities that will form the basis of your lesson, you can analyze the type and quantity of materials and technology that will be needed (Brown, 2007; Jensen, 2001). For instance, if you are presenting new information to learners, you may need a white board and markers, a laptop and projector, pictures, or realia. You may need to copy materials for learners. If so, will you give a copy to each student individually or one copy to each pair or group? Games may necessitate cards, game boards, markers, dice, and prizes. List on your plan the materials you will need and the number of each. If you place this list at the top of your plan, it will be easier for you to refer to as you get ready for class.

Take into consideration that some materials may require advance preparation. For instance, if you wish to use pictures to illustrate new vocabulary, you may have to spend some time searching for appropriate pictures in print materials or on the Internet. You may need to enlarge the pictures or laminate them to make them more useful. If you plan to give a digital presentation using PowerPoint or Prezi, you will have to create it. It can be tempting to grab materials that other teachers have created off the Internet to use in your classes. However, you need to thoroughly read and evaluate these materials to be sure that they meet the objectives of your lesson, are appropriate for your learners, and are of high quality.

Authentic materials are often promoted as being more motivating for students because they represent "real" language as used by native speakers (Gilmore, 2007). If you decide to use authentic materials, you must review them carefully to evaluate whether they are appropriate for your learners with regards to their age, proficiency level, and cultural background. For example, a beer commercial might be suitable to use in a listening exercise for university students in Latin America or Asia, yet it would be highly inappropriate to use a beer commercial with younger learners or with learners in the Middle East. Another consideration with authentic materials is the variety of English represented: British English, North American English, or other varieties of World Englishes. Is this variety of English the variety that your students wish to learn?

Even if you only plan to use exercises from your textbook, these exercises should also be reviewed carefully as you plan your lesson because this will enable you to predict where students will have difficulties. Read the instructions for each activity. Are the instructions clear? Will further instructions to students be necessary? Answer all of the exercises yourself. Do you have difficulty answering any of the prompts? If you do, your students will, too. Check your answers with the answer key. Do you have the same responses as the key, or do multiple responses seem to fit? Be prepared, then, that students will also interpret the prompt in different ways. As you review the textbook exercises, think of how they might be adapted to better meet the needs of your learner population. For instance, your students might have great oral skills but weak literacy skills. Because of this, you may decide to ask students to write their answers to an oral exercise. The textbook is a flexible resource. Be creative in how you use it.

Assessment

As you develop your lesson objectives and procedures, you should also be thinking of how students' learning from this lesson will be assessed (Brown, 2007). How will you know that students have mastered the content or developed the skills that your lesson aims to foster? Perhaps you will use informal methods such as observing and noting students' oral errors or checking their written classwork. Or you may be preparing students to take a formal assessment such as an end-of-course achievement test or a standardized language proficiency exam. If you have used a backward design process (see Chapter 2), assessment will have been a guiding principle in developing the procedures of your lesson. Yet if the form of assessment has not already been determined, you will need to make some further decisions as to how learning will be assessed. For more guidance on assessment practices, refer to *Language Classroom Assessment* (Cheng, 2013).

Another dimension to consider under assessment is the role that error correction and feedback will play in the lesson (Lightbown & Spada, 2013). Will the focus of each activity be more on developing learners' fluency or accuracy? If the focus is on accuracy, which aspects of language will you correct? Grammar? Pronunciation? Word choice? Pragmatic usage? Imagine that you decided that learners' grammatical errors needed to be corrected. Learners can make a large number of errors across a wide range of forms. Will you correct all grammatical errors, or just some of them? If you will only correct some of the errors, which ones will take priority? Making these types of decisions during the lesson planning process will help you to apply error correction more consistently.

Out-of-Class Work

Out-of-class work refers to the learning activities that students engage in outside of class as an extension of the current lesson or in preparation for the coming lesson (Brown, 2007). Make sure that the out-of-class work is meaningful and aids in fulfilling the lesson's objectives. If you are using the flipped lesson model, the out-of-class work that students do (e.g., viewing a video lecture) will serve as the foundation for the activities in the next lesson. Many times teachers are rushed to explain the out-of-class work at the end of the lesson as the bell rings and students begin leaving the classroom. Therefore, be sure to include "Giving instructions for out-of-class work" as part of your procedures, and designate enough time in the lesson to provide adequate instructions and answer students' questions.

Implementing Your Plan

Your lesson has been written, the materials have been gathered, and now it is time to walk into the classroom and implement your plan. Although we may put a lot of effort into developing our lesson plans, it is a rare occasion when our lessons are realized exactly as we have written them! There is almost always some deviation, large or small. Below are some common reasons why lessons do not go as planned:

- Students finish an activity in less time than had been estimated. This may be because the activity was too easy given the students' proficiency level.

- Students need more time to finish an activity than had been estimated. This may be because the activity was too difficult given the students' proficiency level. Other reasons for activities to go "overtime" are because the instructions were not clear and students are confused, or students are not working well together due to personality conflicts.

- Students ask more questions than expected, which extends the time allocated to the presentation of new information.

- Some students are absent, so groups cannot be formed as planned.

- New students enter the class, so groups cannot be formed as planned.

- Students have not completed the out-of-class work necessary to implement the lesson.

- Students express an urgent need to learn language that is unrelated to the lesson objectives, a regular occurrence when teaching adult learners in ESL contexts.

- Technology does not function.

- Administrators interrupt the lesson to make announcements or collect paperwork from students.

- There are emergencies like student illness, electrical outages, or fire drills.

- Students appear bored, do not participate, or exhibit disruptive behaviors.

In all of these cases, the teacher has to make a decision: How should this disruption to the plan be handled? If you find that you have extra time to fill in your lesson, some possibilities are:

- Extending an activity to fill in the extra time in the lesson. If the previous activities leave you with an extra 5–10 minutes, you may allow students to carry on with a planned activity for a bit longer. For example, if students are interviewing each other and the conversation is still active, you could allow them to continue for those extra few minutes. You might also decide to add an additional step to the activity to expand upon it. For instance, in the interview activity, if students have finished conversing, you might then ask them to write a paragraph about their partner.

- Adding an entirely new activity to the lesson. It is always useful to have some extra activities on hand in case you find yourself left with a chunk (10+ minutes) of time when your planned activities have already been completed. Some old standbys are Hangman, Twenty Questions, dictation, and charades. These activities can be adapted to incorporate grammar and vocabulary for different proficiency levels in order to relate to your lesson objectives.

If you find that you have insufficient time to complete your lesson, some courses of action are:

- Reducing the time allotted to an activity. This is a good option if you believe it is important for students to do an activity in order to achieve the lesson objectives. It allows you to meet the objectives while making up for time lost in previous activities. This option may also be necessary for classroom management if students become uncontrollable.

- Eliminating a planned activity from the lesson. This option is viable if you believe the students have already demonstrated mastery of the objectives in the previous activities.

- Continuing on with the lesson as planned and carrying any uncompleted activities into the next lesson. This is a possibility when you know you will have several more lessons on the same topic.

- Throwing out the plan and going with the flow! Of course, this should only occur in extreme cases; for example, an administrator enters the room and announces that everyone in the school must assemble to hear a guest speaker. Otherwise, it will be difficult for you to meet the course goals and for any systematic learning to occur.

Richards and Lockhart (1996) call these and other decisions that the teacher makes as the lesson is in progress "interactive decisions" (p. 83). Interactive decision making involves several different actions:

- Monitoring one's teaching and evaluating what is happening at a particular point in the lesson

- Recognizing that a number of different courses of action are possible

- Selecting a particular course of action

- Evaluating the consequences of the choice (Richards & Lockhart, 1996, p. 84)

REFLECTIVE BREAK

Think of a recent time when you had to deviate from your lesson plan.

- What prompted you to change your plan?

- What type of adjustments did you make?

- What was the result?

Teachers should not blame themselves when lessons do not go as planned. In some cases, such as when learners express an urgent need to learn particular language, the lesson can be more relevant and meaningful for the learners when the plan is left behind. In other cases, it is most important to understand why the lesson could not be implemented as desired (see "Reflecting on Your Plan," below). For instance, perhaps the activity was appropriate for your learners, but you underestimated how much time they would need to complete it. Or maybe you realize that the instructions you gave students were not clear. Consider this a learning experience. Next time, you will be able to make a more accurate estimate of the time your learners will take to complete an activity. Next time, you will take steps to provide clearer instructions, perhaps by scripting out the instructions in your lesson plan or by modeling the activity with the learners before they begin to work on their own. As you gain more experience, your accumulated knowledge of the learners, the curriculum, and the cultural and institutional context in which you work will allow you to write lesson plans that align more and more with the reality of the classroom.

Reflecting on Your Plan

Engaging in the process of lesson planning allows teachers to make conscious decisions about their teaching practice. Once the lesson is over, the written plan acts to document what occurred during the lesson and serves as a stimulus for teacher reflection. Many teachers write notes on their lesson plans to indicate which activities were successful, which were not, and what they would change if the lesson were to be implemented again. What follows is a list of questions to help you reflect on the construction and implementation of your lesson plans.

Learning Objectives

- Did learners understand the objectives of the lesson? If they did not, how could you better communicate the objectives to learners?

- Did the learning activities allow learners to accomplish the learning objectives for this lesson? What evidence do you have that the objectives were accomplished?

- If the learning activities did not allow learners to accomplish the learning objectives, what changes would need to be made to the objectives or to the lesson activities for this to occur?

Materials

- Were the selected instructional materials (e.g., reading passages, grammar exercises) appropriate for the age and proficiency level of the learners?

- Were auxiliary materials (e.g., poster paper, scissors, markers) readily available for this lesson? If not, where can you obtain these in the future?

- Did you have enough materials for all learners to participate?

- Did the technology you employed function correctly? If not, whom should you notify to seek technical assistance?

- Did you know how to use the technology in the classroom? If not, where can you obtain technical training?

Procedures

- If there was a presentation segment in the lesson, how long did it last? Was this amount of information too much information for students or an appropriate amount? If you determine that it was too much information for students, how might the information be divided among multiple lessons in the future?

- Were the selected activities appropriate for the age and proficiency level of the learners?

- Were the activities carried out in an appropriate order? If not, what would be a better sequence of activities?

- Did one activity lead smoothly into the next? If not, how could these transitions be facilitated?

- Did students appear to understand instructions for the activities? If not, how could instructions be made clearer?

- Did the lesson incorporate a variety of formats (i.e., whole class, individual work, pair work, group work)? If not, why not? How could more variety be incorporated within this lesson to achieve the same learning objectives?

- Did all of the students participate? If not, what steps can you take to ensure the participation of all students?

- If pair or group work was used, how were these pairs or groups formed? Would other groupings have been more effective?

- How did this lesson stimulate learners' motivation?

- What options did learners have for processing information or expressing what they know?

- What was the ratio of teacher talk time to student talk time? If this lesson were to be repeated, how could you increase the amount of time students spend using the language?

- What type of interactive decisions did you make during this lesson? What were the outcomes?

Assessment

- If you employed informal assessment during this lesson, how did you document the results?

- If students will be taking a formal assessment based on the content of this lesson, are they adequately prepared for it? If not, how could this lesson be revised to better prepare them? What needs to happen in the next lesson for students to be prepared?

- What types of errors did you notice students making?

- What error correction techniques did you use?

- Did students notice your correction and incorporate the correct form? If not, how might you make your corrections more explicit?

Out-of-Class Work

- Did students do the out-of-class work assigned in preparation for this lesson? If not, what barriers (e.g., motivational, situational, lack of understanding) did learners encounter? How can these barriers be overcome?

General

- What was the greatest strength of this lesson? What was the greatest weakness?

- Did this lesson reflect what you know about second language acquisition, best practices in language teaching, your learners, and the context in which you are working? If not, how can you better align your knowledge with your classroom practice?

Mentally reading through these questions and responding to them in your mind may provide you with some helpful information from one day to the next. However, true reflective practice which would lead to your long-term development as a teacher needs to be more systematic. It would involve collecting data about your lessons and your lesson planning process in order to truly analyze your practice and enact change. For instance, if you maintain a teaching journal, you may choose a question, or cluster of questions, from the above list and use it to stimulate your journal writing, comparing your responses over time. Or if you have access to recording equipment, you might record your lesson and use these questions to analyze the lesson in that format. Please see resources such as Richard and Lockhart (1996) and Farrell (2013) for more information on how to develop your reflective practice as a teacher.

4

Conclusion

As is evident from the discussion presented in this volume, lesson planning is a complex process. There are theoretical issues to consider, such as identifying the foundation of our lesson plan. What is at its core? Is it the content we teach (as it is with forward design), the activities we employ (as it is with central design), or the lesson objectives and their correlating assessments (as it is with backward design)? UDL challenges us to understand that the concept of learner differences implies more than differences in age, proficiency level, and cultural and linguistic background. Learners differ in how they perceive and process information, express their knowledge, and engage in the learning process. UDL provides us with guidelines for addressing this learner variability at all stages of our lessons.

Then, there is the myriad of practical decisions that need to be made for each and every lesson: What are the objectives of our lesson? What activities will we use and at which point in the lesson? How much time should we devote to each? How will students be grouped? What materials are necessary? How will we assess learning? And can we do it all in one class period? Or will we expect students to engage in some out-of-class work? Our teaching practice will be enhanced if we approach these decisions during the lesson planning process; even so, we are often faced with revising these decisions once the lesson is in progress. Having already established a vision for our lesson enables us to make better interactive decisions as we teach. The benefits of lesson planning are numerous, and it is an essential skill that every classroom teacher needs to develop.

References

Bergmann, J., & Sams, A. (2012). *Flip your classroom: Reach every student in every class every day.* Washington, DC: International Society for Technology in Education.

Brown, H. D. (2007). *Teaching by principles: An interactive approach to language pedagogy* (3rd ed.). White Plains, NY: Pearson Longman.

Center for Applied Special Technology. (2011). *Universal Design for Learning guidelines, version 2.0.* Wakefield, MA: Author. Retrieved from http://www.udlcenter.org/aboutudl/udlguidelines/downloads

Cheng, L. (2013). *Language classroom assessment.* Alexandria, VA: TESOL International Association.

Day, R. (2013). *Teaching reading.* Alexandria, VA: TESOL International Association.

Dörnyei, Z., & Ushioda, E. (2010). *Teaching and researching motivation* (2nd ed.). New York, NY: Routledge.

Echevarría, J., Vogt, M. E., & Short, D. J. (2013). *Making content comprehensible for English learners: The SIOP model* (4th ed.). Boston, MA: Pearson.

Farrell, T. S. C. (2013). *Reflective teaching.* Alexandria, VA: TESOL International Association.

Flowerdew, J., & Miller, L. (2005). *Second language listening.* New York, NY: Cambridge University Press.

Gilmore, A. (2007). Authentic materials and authenticity in foreign language learning. *Language Teaching, 40,* 97–118.

Grabe, W., & Stoller, F. (2001). Reading for academic purposes: Guidelines for the ESL/EFL teacher. In M. Celce-Murcia (Ed.), *Teaching English as a second or foreign language* (3rd ed., pp. 187–203). Boston, MA: Heinle Cengage.

Jacobs, G. M., & Kimura, H. (2013). *Cooperative learning and teaching.* Alexandria, VA: TESOL International Association.

Jensen, L. (2001). Planning lessons. In M. Celce-Murcia (Ed.), *Teaching English as a second or foreign language* (3rd ed., pp. 403–413). Boston, MA: Heinle Cengage.

Lightbown, P. M., & Spada, N. (2013). *How languages are learned* (4th ed.). Oxford, United Kingdom: Oxford University Press.

Nemtchinova, E. (2013). *Teaching listening.* Alexandria, VA: TESOL International Association.

Oxford, R. L. (2011). *Teaching and researching language learning strategies.* New York, NY: Routledge.

Reed, M., & Michaud, C. (2010). *Goal-driving lesson planning for teaching English to speakers of other languages.* Ann Arbor, MI: University of Michigan Press.

Richards, J. C. (2001). *Curriculum development in language teaching.* Cambridge, United Kingdom: Cambridge University Press.

Richards, J. C. (2013). Curriculum approaches in language teaching: Forward, central, and backward design. *RELC Journal, 44*(1), 5–33.

Richards, J. C., & Lockhart, C. (1996). *Reflective teaching in second language classrooms.* New York, NY: Cambridge University Press.

Scrivener, J. (2012). *Classroom management techniques.* Cambridge, United Kingdom: Cambridge University Press.

Tomaš, Z., Kostka, I., & Mott-Smith, J. A. (2013). *Teaching writing.* Alexandria, VA: TESOL International Association.

Wiggins, G., & McTighe, J. (2005). *Understanding by design* (Expanded 2nd ed.). Alexandria, VA: Association for Supervision and Curriculum Development.

Willis, D., & Willis, J. (2007). *Doing task-based teaching.* New York, NY: Oxford University Press.

Links to Lesson Plan Templates

K12 Reader — Daily Single Subject Lesson Plan Template
With Grid: Elementary
http://www.k12reader.com/lesson-plan-template-pdfs/elementary-daily
-single-subject-grid.pdf

K12 Reader — Daily Single Subject Lesson Plan Template: Secondary
http://www.k12reader.com/lesson-plan-template-pdfs/secondary-daily
-single-subject.pdf

The English Genie — Printable Lesson Plan Template
http://englishgenie.com/wp-content/uploads/2013/03/lesson-plan
-template.pdf

ESL Kid Stuff — Lesson Plan Template (full version)
http://www.eslkidstuff.com/resources/lesson-plan-template-01.pdf

Appendix

Sample Lesson Plan (high-school aged,
high-beginning proficiency class
in an EFL environment)

Objectives

At the end of the lesson, students will be able to

- Make statements about personal life experiences in their past using regular and irregular verbs in simple past tense.

- Ask questions about the previous life experiences of others.

- Write five sentences about their past experience using regular and irregular verbs in simple past tense.

Materials

- White board and white board marker for the teacher.

- Large sheets of white paper, cut into strips, one for each student.

- A permanent marker for each student.

- A timeline with events from the country's history with copies for each student.

Procedure

Grouping	Activity	Time (minutes)
Whole class	(Opening) The teacher presents the lesson objectives to students.	1
Whole class	The teacher reviews the rules for forming past time verbs studied in prior lessons.	9
Whole class	The teacher explains to students what a *timeline* is and how it is arranged in chronological order. The teacher draws a timeline on the board that reflects important events in his or her life. The students listen as the teacher tells the class about his or her life, pointing to the dates on the timeline as a reference. Students are encouraged to ask the teacher questions about his or her experiences.	10
Individuals	The teacher distributes the long slips of paper and markers to the students. Students should draw a timeline that represents at least five important dates in their own lives.	10
Whole class	Students stand up and form a line based on the order of their birthdays (January 1–December 31). Students need to ask each other "When were you born?" and answer "I was born on (date)" in order to form the line. Once in line, each student states his or her birthday in order to check the accuracy of the line. They then form a pair with the person next to them in the line. If there are an odd number of students, one group of three may be necessary.	5
Pairs	In pairs, students tell each other orally about their past experiences, using their timelines as a reference. Students are encouraged to ask each other questions.	10
Individuals	Students return to their own chairs and write five sentences about the past experiences represented in their timelines.	10

Procedure *(continued)*

Grouping	Activity	Time (minutes)
Whole class	Teacher asks students to turn in their sentences. (Closing) Teacher reviews the lesson objectives and gives an overview of the next lesson.	2
Whole class	Teacher distributes a timeline with important dates from that country's history. For homework, students write five sentences about the history of their country.	3

Assessment

The teacher will know if students have met the objectives by monitoring their individual oral responses, monitoring their oral pair work, and checking the sentences they have written in class and for homework. The midterm exam will require students to write sentences in simple past tense. Error correction will focus on the accuracy of simple past time verbs with regards to form (spelling and pronunciation), meaning, and use.

Out-of-Class Work

At the end of class, the teacher distributes the timeline with important dates in the country's history. At home, students write five sentences about the history of their country.

Also Available in the English Language Teacher Development Series

. . . *AND MORE* . . .

www.tesol.org/bookstore
tesolpubs@brightkey.net
Request a copy for review
Request a Distributor Policy